WISE MATING

Abhijit Naskar is one of twenty-first century's most influential minds in Neuroscience and an untiring advocate of global harmony and peace. He became a beloved best-selling author all over the world with his very first book "The Art of Neuroscience in Everything", that heralded the advent of a beautiful scientific philosophy. With various of his pioneering ventures into the Neuropsychology of religious sentiments, he has hugely contributed to humanity's attempt of diminishing religious differences, for which he is popularly hailed as a humanitarian who incessantly works towards taking the human civilization in the path of sweet general harmony.

WISE MATING

A TREATISE ON
MONOGAMY

ABHIJIT NASKAR

Wise Mating: A Treatise on Monogamy

Copyright © 2017 Abhijit Naskar

This is a work of non-fiction

An Amazon Publishing Company, 1st Edition, 2017

Printed in United States of America

ISBN-13: 978-1546817598

Also by Abhijit Naskar

The Art of Neuroscience in Everything
Your Own Neuron: A Tour of Your Psychic Brain
The God Parasite: Revelation of Neuroscience
The Spirituality Engine
Love Sutra: The Neuroscientific Manual of Love
Homo: A Brief History of Consciousness
Neurosutra: The Abhijit Naskar Collection
Autobiography of God: Biopsy of A Cognitive Reality
Biopsy of Religions: Neuroanalysis towards Universal
Tolerance
Prescription: Treating India's Soul
What is Mind?
In Search of Divinity: Journey to The Kingdom of Conscience
Love, God & Neurons: Memoir of a scientist who found
himself by getting lost
The Islamophobic Civilization: Voyage of Acceptance
Neurons of Jesus: Mind of A Teacher, Spouse & Thinker
Neurons, Oxygen & Nanak
The Education Decree
Principia Humanitas
The Krishna Cancer
Rowdy Buddha: The First Sapiens
We Are All Black: A Treatise on Racism
The Bengal Tigress: A Treatise on Gender Equality
Either Civilized or Phobic: A Treatise on Homosexuality

To My Companion Lizi.

You make me a better man, a better human, a better scientist and a better philosopher.

CONTENTS

1.
What is Monogamy

We humans are fascinating creatures. We cannot live alone. We cannot bear solitude. We love independence, yet at the same time, we desire to be with someone, only to lose a part of that very independence. We crave for freedom, yet we crave even more to have someone next to us, to share that freedom with.

When two people fall in love, they not only give up their genuine authority over their own lives, but also, they become mutual authorities of the collective life that they build together. These collective lives collectively make the most of our human society.

It is like human life has no value in it, unless you get to share it with someone. Every joy, every agony, every outburst of emotions, that you experience, you do not experience it alone, but equally with your partner. Every joy has two shares in it. Every sorrow has two shares in it. Every success has two shares in it. Every failure has two shares in it. That's how the most part of a civilization is built.

A healthy civilization is built upon the edifice of healthy families. And a healthy family is built upon the foundation of four legs, two belonging to each individual. It does not matter, whether these four legs belong to individuals with opposite sex orientation or same sex orientation. What matters is the bond between these two individuals. When this bond is not strong enough the legs tremble, and so does the family built upon them. And when many such families keep trembling, it can rock the soul of a civilization. This, my friend, is called Monogamy – which is not about the wellbeing of an individual, but about the wellbeing of a civilization.

2.
Is it natural

Monogamy is no more unnatural than refraining from pedophilia. Monogamy is no more unnatural than refraining from incest. Monogamy is no more unnatural than refraining from being a racist. There are certain moralistic tenets that define the true nature of a civilized world. And monogamy is one of those crucial tenets.

Yes you will have desires to have sex with as many partners as possible - men more so, than women. Yes you will have your libido humming whenever you see a charming person - men more so, than women. But that does not mean, a civilized person will act on these primitive impulses of the limbic system.

A healthy world is made of healthy nations. A healthy nation is made of healthy families. And a healthy family can only be raised on the foundation of a monogamous relationship. However, if we were the bonobos, we would not worry about it so much, because the bonobos have sex with every other bonobo they come across in their community. But we are not bonobos - are we? We are humans. It means, we have the cortical capacity to keep our impulses in check. We have highly developed frontal lobes that give rise to a functioning conscience. And this conscience tells us, that by acting upon the libidinal impulse of mating with every charming person we meet, we would not only jeopardize a healthy and happy communion, but also we would hurt the person closest to us, who has been there with us in our joys and sorrows.

However, if one wants to swing around the rest of his or her life, and not to raise a family, then it is perfectly okay to have a promiscuous lifestyle. But promiscuity is no sign of taking the revolutionary next step of human sexual behavior. Promiscuity is all about sexual satisfaction. But monogamy is far beyond the mere cravings of genitals. Monogamy is about an all-pervading mental contentment. It is as simple as this - polygamy is about sex, whereas monogamy is about love. Monogamy is about a wide array of emotions - it is about values - it is about being an inseparable part of somebody's soul.

Monogamy is one of the core foundations of being civilized humans, at least for those who desire to raise a family. It is not a social construct - it is an evolutionary trait of the majority of individuals of a species, looking to propagate their genes in a healthy fashion. And of course, there are always some individuals who do not have a desire to make babies, for whatever reason. These individuals may choose to be promiscuous, and would still remain an essential part of the civilized human society, as long as they do have a functional conscience to say no to advances from individuals in monogamous relationships. Either one is promiscuous or in a relationship - it cannot be both at the same time. If a person is consistently engaged in both a committed relationship and promiscuity at the same time, then that person is no civilized human - but a mockery of "humanhood".

And those who boastfully comment that polygamy or promiscuity is natural and monogamy is not, to them I shall point out - being evil is natural, being good is not - being superstitious is natural, being rational is not - being selfish is natural, being compassionate is not - being racist is natural, being humanist is not. Yet these qualities, which can be viewed as unnatural from the standpoint of the advocates of promiscuity, are the ones that determine whether we have really advanced in the path of genuine intellectual progress, or we still remain barbarian cave-people with no conscientious control over the primitive impulses of our mind.

What is natural, needs to be looked upon, scrutinized and reshaped by each generation of the world, to make it compatible with the path of progress of a civilized society. For example, slavery on the grounds of racial discrimination was hailed as natural in many parts of the Western World, until about a century ago. Today, after rigorous struggle most of us have become civilized enough to see all humans as equal, even though our limbic system elicits an implicit response of fear and anxiety when we visualize dark skin. We can do this, because the frontal lobes of our brain enable us to be truly rational while having a functional control over any conscious or subconscious fear response that may rise from the primitive parts of our mind. Hence, we can feel, think and behave as rational, conscientious and civilized beings. If this is unnatural, then we need more of these unnatural traits my friend, to become truly human.

The point is, if any person thinks that every emotional impulse that rises in the mind naturally, is morally acceptable and justifiable, then that person has to rethink about his or her entire perception of moral parameters. Such a callous notion would only lead to a chaotic world with no order, peace and wellbeing in both the individual and social aspects of life. Let me give you a little example to elucidate on this matter. When a man gets mad at his wife, he gets extremely close to hitting her, driven by his natural impulse of rage. Here, from the standpoint of doing what comes naturally, one may gloriously say that, since the impulse of hitting his wife comes naturally, why resist it at all - why not simply hit her! Because, my friend - that is not human. Not all internal impulses are morally right - not all feelings that float around the mind are civilized - and above all, not all elements of emotions are signs of "humanhood".

Being human means having an active filter mechanism to distinguish between the right and the wrong. And in no world, assaulting the person you love, can be hailed as right and civilized, at least by the genuine humans. We developed our advanced cortical capacities for a reason. And it is to keep such momentary primitive impulses in check for a healthy and happy life. Sex is only a tiny part of this entire process of health and happiness. It is a process that influences all aspects of human life at a molecular level of the anatomy.

In fact, upon the edifice of this process, a life is constructed. And self-restraint is an essential part of this process. It is a quintessential mental mechanism that sustains the wellbeing of the human life. A man squanders his money on gambling. A woman beats her child. A drunk driver causes a crash that destroys three cars and injures several pedestrians. A student postpones studying until the night before the test and gets a bad grade. A young couple engages in unprotected sex and creates an unwanted pregnancy. A delinquent shoots an acquaintance during an argument. A girl breaks a promise and betrays a friend's confidence. What these disparate events have in common is failure of self-restraint or self-regulation. When self-regulation works well, it enables people to alter their behavior so as to conform to promises, ideals, values and other standards of human life. When it fails, a broad range of human problems and misfortunes can arise. Self-regulation is thus a key to wellbeing in human life.

Self-regulation is not simply a moral characteristic. It is biologically healthy for both your mind and the body. Which means, those who practice self-restraint have better physical and psychological health. Countless studies have revealed that people with high scores on self-control were better off than those with low self-control on virtually everything. They had better grades in school. They had better relationships with family and friends - less conflict and more cohesion. They were better able to understand others and scored higher on empathy. They showed better psychological adjustment, including fewer psychological problems, fewer signs of serious psychopathology, and higher self-esteem. Not surprisingly, they reported fewer impulse control problems, such as overeating and problem drinking. They had healthier emotional lives, such as being better at managing their anger, and being more prone to guilt than shame. They had less juvenile delinquency.

Other work using the same scale has confirmed the benefits. Supervisors who score higher in self-control are rated more favorably (e.g., as fairer) by their subordinates. People with high self-control make better relationship partners, especially because they are better able to adapt to partners. The most dramatic and conclusive evidence of the long-term benefits of self-regulation comes from the research by Walter Mischel and his colleagues.

Mischel was a pioneer of self-regulation research because of his studies on delay of gratification, beginning in the 1960s. Self-regulation is required to override the impulse to seek immediate gratification in order to obtain greater but delayed rewards. His research group followed up the early studies, which were typically done with young children, to see how they fared on into adulthood. Four and five year olds who were able to resist the temptation of one cookie in order to eat two cookies a short while later grew up to earn better marks on the SAT, to be rated by others as rational and socially competent, and to cope with frustration and stress better than those kids who were relatively unable to resist the tempting cookie at a young age. Thus, effective self-regulation can be recognized as an important key to "success" in life.

Cheating in relationship is a sign of self-regulation failure. When it happens ones, it is a mistake. When it happens twice, it is unfortunate. But when it happens thrice or more, it is a pattern indicating primitive, uncivilized inhuman behavior. Such a behavior cannot be a justifiable trait of the civilized society. Such a behavior only makes sense in a society of savages, not of modern humans. Committing to a relationship, means consenting to become the vehicle of each other's physical and mental gratification. And in that commitment self-regulation makes a deep contribution, especially in the long run.

Sometimes, humanity surprises me with all its lack of control over the primordial urges. These innate urges are the biological traits that make us similar to the rest of the animal kingdom. But the modern qualities that make us superior to all the animals are intellect and self-control. So, even though it is true that deep within, we are still unconsciously the same old cave-people or simply wild animals craving for sexual satisfaction, we also have developed the neurological capability to keep those instincts in check for a healthier and happier life and society.

And due to obvious evolutionary reason, men are more primordial in the domain of sexual pursuit. For a man, the optimal evolutionary strategy is to disseminate his genes as widely as possible, given his few minutes or, alas, seconds, of investment in each encounter. While on the contrary, a woman invests a great deal of time and effort - a nine month long, risky, strenuous pregnancy, in each offspring.

Naturally, over the course of millions of years, women have evolved into a more monogamous creature than men, while on the other hand, the tendency of men is to be polygamous and promiscuous. Now the question that may rise in your mind is, if men are biologically more polygamous and women are more monogamous, then how can a romantic relationship ever last for long?

The answer is in the evolution of various brain regions. It is true that men will always be men with their innate wild attraction towards large breasts and big hips even while being in a relationship. But through the process of Natural Selection, an amazing brain region evolved inside the skull - the prefrontal cortex. Our very civilized qualities are predicated on the healthy functioning of the Prefrontal Cortex.

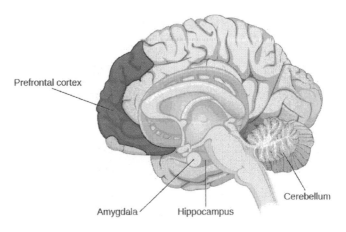

Figure 2.1 Prefrontal Cortex shown as darker region. A healthy prefrontal cortex means better emotional stability.

Prefrontal cortex is the area of the brain that gives you the ability to keep all your momentary emotional impulses in check. It is a small portion in the front part of the cerebral cortex. The entire cerebral cortex is the crowning achievement of primate evolution. It is the constructor of all the your inexplicable and typically human faculties. It is the part of the brain that most distinctively sets us apart from any other species on this planet. And the architect of the cerebral cortex, like all other biological mechanism, is Mother Nature herself.

By putting selective pressure over the hominin brain, Mother Nature made the human brain circuits go through not only quantitative but also qualitative changes, over the period of a few million years. And these changes are most significant in the Cerebral Cortex. In fact, the principles governing the cortical development hold the key to understanding our cognitive capacity of intelligence and creativity.

You must remember, that all your pride of being superior to all other animals on earth, is because of the Cerebral Cortex. Without the highly advanced and complicated neural network of the cortex, there is no difference between us and other animals.

The human cerebral cortex is a laminated structure composed of the most bewildering diversity of neurons arranged in distinct patterns among all the species on earth. We are what we are because of this diversity of neurons in the cerebral cortex. This diversity enables us to become the most advanced as well as civilized species on this planet. However, the human mind also has a neurological predisposition to act in profoundly wild and uncivilized ways. And all our primitive aboriginal urges emerge from this innate predisposition of monstrosity.

This primitive version of our mind lies within the deepest region of the human brain. This region is much more ancient than the modern cerebral cortex of the civilized human mind. It is the Limbic System, that lies right below the layers of the cerebral cortex.

Most of the limbic brain has been there since our reptilian days. The face of this ancient region of the brain is shameless and ill-mannered. It is a wild beast that does not play well with any kind of social norms, unlike the civilized face of the cerebral cortex. These two faces of your mind are completely opposite of each other, yet they work together to keep you up on your feet. It is the fascinating interplay between the Cerebral Cortex and Limbic System, that makes us civilized human beings with heaps of emotions and values.

Like all other mental and physical faculties of the human species, the cortical control over emotions evolved out of a growing need to survive in the dreadful environment of the wilderness. It began with our Australopithecine ancestors who lived around three millions years ago. They had just left the forest and moved to the savanna where their upright posture helped to see longer distances for scavenging food and watching for predators.

While living in the harsh environment of the wild, a very important tool of survival was being next to each other. This is what we call social organization. And our Australopithecine ancestors had a kind of basic social organization. The freaky surrounding compelled the Australopithecines to live in groups. Once they started to live in groups, they required further social skills in order to manage their social relationship, which in turn proved to be an important trigger for the increase in the brain size. By developing social skills the Australopithecines formed alliances and coalitions within the group in order to supervise their survival inside their society as well as outside of it.

With the limited cranial capacity of about 500 cc, the Australopithecines did indeed encounter the dawn of human consciousness. They were still very much primitive, at the same time they were primitively conscious. They developed a kind of emotional communication, which was confined to physical gestures and primitive vocalization. But, such communication system had its own headache. Any negative emotional outbreak could disrupt harmony in the group. Such emotional outbreaks were followed by a lot of noises which attracted attention of the predators. Naturally, this created an adaptive pressure for cortical control of emotion and for the so-called basic social emotions of sympathy, guilt, and shame which promote cohesiveness. This triggered an increase in the brain size which was mostly in the neocortex that added an extra layer to the whole brain and made room for more neurons. Their primitive form of social organization influenced the human brain to embark on an evolutionary journey of becoming the most social, emotional and advanced brain on planet Earth.

The limbic system constructs all the emotional elements of your mental universe, which are then imposed on your conscious mind after passing through the cortical gateway of moderation under the watch of the Prefrontal Cortex in the Frontal Lobes of the Cerebral Cortex.

So, even though a man is biologically incapable of ceasing his testosterone level to go high when he visualizes a hot lady, he still can choose whether to act upon that momentary impulse of libido, by practicing the healthy functioning of his prefrontal cortex. In fact, if he is in a relationship he can utilize this situation to his best interest, by channeling that momentary surge of lust and slowly shifting the focus on his own partner. Once the body is turned on, it no longer matters whether the satisfaction is coming from the same source that triggered the turn on in the first place. So, it is a fantastic opportunity to add some kink to the relationship.

Hence, to a man I say - when life gives you lemons, you should make lemonade out of 'em, and when a situation gives you testosterone surges, you might as well make some bed-bursting consummation out of 'em.

Every man is subconsciously promiscuous, but it is the conscious mind that keeps those primordial urges in check. A healthy brain creates a healthy mind, which keeps your relationship strong, safe and healthy.

Some people, nay animals, however, even while being in a relationship, most shamelessly attempt to justify their lack of self-control over the primitive libidinal impulses with sophisticated terms like "monogamish" etc. This simply means they love their partner, but not enough to commit entirely to that partner and would be most happy to sleep with every other attractive person that comes along the way. They most blatantly promote swinging, philandering and all sorts of primordial actions which in no way are signs of a civilized and wise conscience.

Promoting promiscuity in this evolved and civilized society is actually like signing the Declaration, that says:

"I hereby renounce my membership of humankind, since I am neither human nor kind. I declare that I no longer belong to the modern human species, i.e. the Homo sapiens. From now on I shall be counted among the swingers of the animal kingdom, such as the bonobo or montane vole. I am simply an arrogant philandering savage."

Philanderers and swingers can see nothing beyond the needs of their genitals. Sexual craving is a part of our biology, but it is not who we are. We are a unique combination of intellect and emotions, of which genital desire is only a tiny portion. And this combination is what makes us human. But the philandering creatures, not unlike the religious fundamentalists, are not qualified to be entitled as "human", because both these creatures tend to drag the human civilization back to the barbarian times. Being human means being wise. And wisdom means winning over the internal evil, not giving in to it. Being open minded is good, but not so open that you lose the moral compass to distinguish the civilized from the savage.

Morality of a civilized human leads to monogamy, even though it is not easy. Monogamy is about romantic relationship, whereas there is no such thing as polygamous romantic relationship, because polygamy is all about individual sexual gratification with no element of sacrifice involved. And, if you are not sacrificing a part of yourself in a relationship, then you are not in a relationship.

A relationship is not just about sex – it is much more than that. Sex is only a tool in love, not love itself. True love is born out of the pyre of two committed souls. And it is not only a pleasurable phenomenon, but also a healthy one. It is a phenomenon that elicits mutual physiological and psychological benefits in two people, and thereafter their children. In this aspect, polygamy or the so-called "open relationship" is not much different from being single, even though it involves much more momentary spikes in both gratification and depression than being single. In comparison with both polygamy and singlehood, monogamy is the midway and the healthiest way.

I further deduce, in terms of raising a family, two monogamous parents are better than a single parent who may or may not be looking for a lasting relationship. But neither of these two parental environments is harmful to the children. On the contrary, promiscuous (having multiple sexual relationships) or polygamous (having multiple spouses) parents are downright harmful to the developing psyche of the children. A philanderer cannot be a parent - a parent cannot be a philanderer.

Polygamy is a so-called marital relationship involving multiple spouses and occurs in several forms. The most common form of polygamy occurs when a man has more than one wife at the same time, known as polygyny. Less frequently, it occurs when a woman has more than one husband (polyandry) and when more than one husband is married to more than one wife (polygynandry). Polygamy is legally practised in various countries in the Middle East, Asia and Africa, although not practised by the civilized ones. Factors affecting the occurrence of polygamy include social, economic and religious factors.

Most research on polygamy, especially polygyny, has focused on the adults rather than the children in the family, particularly the wives. Countless studies on the effects of polygyny on women has found detrimental effects on the mental health of wives. Also, limited research on husbands in polygynous marriages has found that polygyny can be detrimental to husbands.

Research on children in polygynous families has revealed that family structure is important for child and adolescent development. Among the various family structures experienced by children, polygynous family structures have received less research attention from psychologists. However, much of the research has identified negative outcomes for children, including academic outcomes as well as psychological outcomes such as internalizing problems, externalizing problems and mental health problems.

Family variables and risk factors associated with polygyny that could influence children's developmental outcomes include marital conflict, marital distress, father absence, the happiness or distress of the wives in polygynous marriages, financial stress and parental education.

Studies have distinctly revealed that polygamy has detrimental effects on children and adolescents. When compared to children from monogamous families, children from polygynous families had a variety of problems such as mental health disorders, scholastic difficulties and social problems. None of the studies on this matter reported benefits of polygyny for children.

Also, there is a thing called serial monogamy, which means one may have multiple partners throughout the lifespan but only in a monogamous relationship, i.e. one partner at a time. In this type of scenario, to ensure the proper mental and physical development of the child a couple should make every possible effort to stay together without being hostile to each other at least during the first decade of a child's life.

Monogamous marriage results in significant improvements in child welfare, including lower rates of child neglect, abuse, accidental death, homicide and intra-household conflict. These benefits result from greater levels of parental investment, smaller households and increased direct "blood relatedness" in monogamous family households. In short, monogamy leads to a healthy and happy family.

It takes genuine effort from both partners, but it is totally worth it. On the contrary, polygamy, promiscuity, philandering, swinging, all these primitive practices lead to a broken home, from both mental and physiological aspects. These practices are not only harmful to the wellbeing of the human society, but also, in time, they lead to an existential crisis of the entire species. Therefore, monogamy is not merely a construct of our moral values but a quintessential element of a healthy civilization. It is not a choice, it is a responsibility of a genuine human. The other healthy alternative is being single.

The point is, courtship and mating are risky, requiring that both partners venture out of their personal shell and become vulnerable to rejection, injury, bad choices, or just plain wasting of energy. Having done so once and succeeded in obtaining a gratifying mate, the healthiest and most rational decision is to stop such risky prospecting and settle down to a life of cozy, comfortable domesticity.

Having found a reliable and mutually gratifying relationship, why ruin it, my friend, especially if you intend to raise a family? It has been documented among animals, including humans, that the longer pairs are together, the more likely they are to be successful at rearing offspring. This is because experience and familiarity with each other, make for better and more efficient parenting. The more you get familiar with each other, the better you become at being parents and providing a healthy environment for your kids. Thus, spouses who know each other well make great parents. Also, a marriage rewires your entire neuroanatomy in such a way, that people who are happily married live longer and healthier than either divorced people or those who are unhappily married.

A healthy marriage acts as the vessel of wellbeing and stability for both partners as well as the children. It is a social construct, founded upon the natural phenomenon of love, which happens to be a healthy one, unlike some other harmful social constructs, such as racial and gender-based discriminations. Marriage is in fact, one of the healthiest social constructs of the civilized society.

3.
Is it Evolutionary

Survival of a species is predicated on its reproductive success. But simply mating does not guarantee successful procreation. A lot more effort needs to be invested by the parents to actually ensure the survival of their progeny. For us humans, this can be up to twenty years. For this purpose, Mother Nature developed strategies beyond the "one time fling" approach to make mating partners collaborate until their progeny can survive on its own. Hence the neurological circuits of pair-bonding evolved. Along the way, it led to the neuropsychological arrival of monogamy as a favored type of relationship. However, scientifically speaking, women tend to be more monogamous than men, whereas the tendency of men is to be polygamous and promiscuous.

For a man, the optimal evolutionary strategy is to disseminate his genes as widely as possible, given his few minutes, or, alas, seconds, of investment in each encounter. It all makes simple evolutionary sense, since a woman invests a good deal of time and effort - a nine month long, risky, strenuous pregnancy, in each offspring. Naturally she has to be very discerning in her choice of sexual partners.

And as said in the previous chapter - men will always be men with their innate wild attraction to new sexual stimuli, such as all the breasts and hips they encounter in their everyday walk of life, even while being in a relationship, but that does not mean they do not have the choice of whether or not to act upon that attraction. They do have the choice – we all have the choice. Because we have a fully functional Prefrontal Cortex that makes us real civilized humans.

Just imagine the concern that Mother Nature has for us, rhetorically speaking (here I must clear something up - we biologists often use the phrase "Mother Nature" to refer to the entire system of Nature that we see around us, but it is not really an entity, and it does not have any real concern for any of its living creatures – it lives on with or without us; it is in our human psychology to impose a human-like identity upon any grand system that we encounter around us – it gives us a sense of closeness to that system and makes us feel an essential part of it). Mother Nature put all her excellence in designing various brain circuits with utmost care so that we could lead a healthy, happy and abundant family life (when I say, Mother Nature designed us, or programmed us, I am simply referring to the process of natural selection). She programmed us to go crazy with just a glance of our beloved ones.

In various studies we have found that merely having a look at the picture of your dear ones turns on various regions of the brain such as the insula, anterior cingulate cortex, putamen, retrosplenial cortex and caudate, like a nuclear furnace. The insula and anterior cingulate cortex are typically associated with emotion-oriented attentional states, whereas the retrosplenial cortex is involved in episodic memory recall, imagination, and planning for the future.

And of course, the brain's love circuits share several brain regions with sexual arousal circuits. In several studies, it has been found that certain regions do appear to be consistently heightened in response to sexual stimuli, such as the hypothalamus, putamen, visual cortex, inferior temporal cortex, orbitofrontal cortex, anterior cingulate cortex, parietal cortex, temporo-parietal junction, insula, ventral striatum, anterior temporal areas, amygdala, and basal ganglia. These studies have also pointed out a few regions that are distinctively active only in response to romantic stimuli. And those regions are caudate and ventral tegmental area. This significantly implies that the brain circuits of love and sexual arousal are anatomically distinctive yet intertwined.

But the craftsmanship of nature does not end just here. Like a nourishing mother, she embedded the ingredients of attachment right inside our head. Those ingredients are Oxytocin and Vasopressin. They play a critical role in forming a concept of our partner whom we want to be with. They appear to build a strong profile of the mating partner through odor. The odor comes to be associated with a pleasurable and rewarding encounter with a particular partner. The same works in the visual domain. Oxytocin is not only responsible for the bonding of couples but also it is involved in maternal love towards a baby, whereas vasopressin is responsible for the commitment of the male towards his mate.

But the brain region activation in women that correlates with maternal love is not identical to the one with romantic love. An interesting distinction lies in the strong activation of fusiform gyrus that is involved in the attention to faces in maternal love. This counts for the importance of reading children's facial expressions to ensure their well-being. This leads to the constant attention that a mother pays to the face of her child. Damage or abnormality in the fusiform gyrus leads to the condition called "prosopagnosia" or simply "face blindness". Another interesting difference is the hypothalamus, which is involved in sexual arousal, thus only in romantic love.

The influence of Oxytocin and Vasopressin is far more delicate than you can imagine. These two incredible hormones go to great length to keep us from being promiscuous. To illustrate this, let me tell you the story of the prairie and the montane voles. It is a story of great biological interest. Among these two species, the prairie voles are mostly monogamous in nature, while the montane voles are promiscuous. Due to their brain circuits, the montane voles cannot maintain a healthy long-term relationship. If the release of Oxytocin and Vasopressin is blocked in prairie voles, they too become promiscuous. If however prairie voles are injected with these hormones but prevented from having sex, they will still continue to be faithful to their partners through a chaste monogamous relationship. That makes me wonder, what if we just inject the montane voles with Oxytocin and Vasopressin! Makes sense right!

One might think that injecting the montane voles with these two hormones will somehow magically transform them into faithful monogamous creatures. But quite unfortunately it doesn't work that way. An injection of these "love potions" as I call them, don't render them monogamous. Once secreted by the pituitary, these neurochemicals can only act if there are receptors for them in the brain. In the prairie voles there is an abundance of receptors for Oxytocin and Vasopressin in the reward centers of the brain. While on the contrary in the montane voles, receptors for these two hormones are not as abundant. Ergo, injecting the montane voles with excessive amounts of Oxytocin and Vasopressin doesn't make them monogamous, since there are not sufficient receptors for them in the reward centers.

There is a genetic cause behind this receptor variability. Prairie voles carry a longer version of the vasopressin receptor gene which makes them way more monogamous in behavior than the montane voles. Our two closest primate cousins, chimpanzees and bonobos also have different lengths of this gene, which match their social behaviors especially in the sexual aspect. Chimpanzees, who have the shorter gene, live in territorially based societies controlled by males who make frequent, fatal war raids on neighboring troops. While on the other hand, bonobos are run by female hierarchies and seal every social interaction with a bit of sexual impression. They are exceptionally social and have the long version of the gene.

Bonobos are a uniquely promiscuous species. They live by the code "make love, not war", quite literally. Sex is the key to the social life of the bonobos. Bonobos become sexually aroused remarkably easily, and they express this excitement in a variety of mounting positions and genital contacts. Although chimpanzees virtually never adopt face-to-face positions, bonobos do so in one out of three copulations in the wild. Furthermore, the frontal orientation of the bonobo vulva and clitoris strongly suggest that the female genitalia are adapted for this position.

The most unique sexual behavior in bonobos is genito-genital rubbing between adult females. One female facing another clings with arms and legs to a partner that, standing on both hands and feet, lifts her off the ground. The two females then rub their genital swellings together, emitting grins and squeals that reflect orgasmic experiences.

Male bonobos, too, may engage in pseudocopulation but generally perform a variation. Standing back to back, one male briefly rubs his scrotum against the buttocks of another. They also practice "penis-fencing", in which two males hang face to face from a branch while rubbing their erect penises together.

The diversity of erotic contacts in bonobos includes sporadic oral sex, massage of another individual's genitals and intense tongue-kissing. The sexual activity of bonobos is rather casual and relaxed, and appears to be a completely natural part of their group life. Like people, bonobos engage in sex only occasionally, not continuously. Furthermore, with the average copulation lasting 13 seconds, sexual contact in bonobos is rather quick by human standards.

The human version of the vasopressin receptor gene is more like the bonobo gene. Differences in partner commitment may therefore be related to our individual differences in the length of this gene and in hormones. However, unlike bonobos or indeed any other animal, the humans have a well-developed cerebral cortex, which endows us with the typically human faculties of conscience and self-control. It enables us to choose whether or not to act upon the innate primordial urge of promiscuity. Those who make genuine efforts to keep those urges in control are the ones with a great character, and the rest are just plain cave-people.

Today you can see, a lot of successful men, especially those in power, cheat on their women, and from this there has emerged a certain notion that cheating or promiscuity is perhaps natural and acceptable. But in reality, success does not define character. A successful person is not necessarily a good person. A good person is the one who can distinguish between the right and wrong, and who learns from his or her mistakes, like a real human being. And it is the good people who are qualified to take the society in the path of genuine healthy progress, not the successful animals who look like humans.

Also remember, technological advancement does not bring genuine progress until it is paired with intellectual and moral advancement. First develop the mind, then the world, otherwise, you will bring destruction upon the world without even being aware of it. For any species to become truly advanced in both physical and mental aspects, it must first recognize the self. And till now, it is only the humans who have the faculty to do so. Do not let that faculty be wasted only in the pursuit of developing mindless machines. We need machines, but more than that we need humans who know how to use those machines for the greater good. We need technology, but more than that we need humans who know how to use that technology to ensure the wellbeing of the human society. Now is the time that we need such humans more than ever, for Mother Earth is wailing for peace. She is wailing for harmony. And she is patiently waiting to behold her adolescent humans, to grow up into loving, conscientious and courageous adults.

4.
What is Marriage

Marriage is the communion of two committed souls who are passionate about each other. And as such, monogamy and marriage go hand in hand, not polygamy and marriage. However, monogamy can thrive without marriage, but a true marriage cannot survive without monogamy. In the society of civilized humans, there can be no such thing as an "open marriage" or "polygamous marriage", because no human being in the right mind who is passionate about his or her partner, would remain undisturbed to share the partner with somebody else. If someone says he or she is completely comfortable with letting the partner sleep with other people, it means that he or she is not passionate about the relationship at all, at least beyond the primitive domain of sexual gratification. A society full of polygamous marriages is as primeval and dangerous as a society full of racists, misogynists and xenophobes.

Here one may proudly come up with the notion that marriage is merely a social construct, so why give importance to it at all. The answer is, marriage is indeed a social construct, but it is a construct based on the biological trait of pair-bonding. And this specific social construct, unlike the primeval construct of racial discrimination, provides stability in the society. Some constructs of the society are indeed harmful to peace and progress, and require reshaping or elimination, but not all. Marriage is a social construct but a healthy one.

Now one might wonder, if it is so healthy, why does it fail so often in todays' society? In most cases, a marriage fails not due to the lack of love, but due to the lack of understanding – it fails due to the lack of insight of each other's mental world. Over time this lack of insight makes a person begin to take his or her partner for granted, and thereafter look outside the marriage for a supposedly better prize. Thus, true love hits the ground so hard that it is often almost impossible to revived it.

Remember, true love is not something you find. You have to build it with the person in whose eyes you see your soul. And once you successfully build that intimate world of love and trust with your partner, never in any circumstances give up on it. It is always easier to give up in search of a better prize, because the brain always keeps craving for new stimuli, but this way you only keep on searching, never to find peace and contentment in life. Few moments of libidinal gratification are not worth compromising the trust of the person who holds you most dear.

Let me tell you a story. There was a student who asked his teacher, what is love? The teacher said go into the field and bring me the most beautiful flower. The student returned with no flower at hand and said, "I found the most beautiful flower in the field but I didn't pick it up for I might find a better one, but when I returned to the place, it was gone."

We always look for the best in life. When we finally see it, we take it for granted and after some time start expecting a better one, not knowing that it's the best for us. Do not seek for the best partner, but seek for the person who makes you a better version of yourself and once you find the one, never ever give up on you both, no matter the situations.

In order to reveal the utter significance of understanding in a romantic relationship, let me bring up a thought experiment entitled "The PMDD Conundrum" which I proposed in the chapter "Free Will" of my book "What is Mind?".

THE PMDD CONUNDRUM (THOUGHT EXPERIMENT)

Mental health influences your decision-making ability regardless of your experiences. However, experience is what makes you better at making the right decision in a given situation. Here the term right only refers to your subjective perspective of the choice. To explain how experience alters one's free will, let's carry out a little thought experiment in the context of two different scenarios.

CONTEXT 1

Imagine yourself to be layman with no notable awareness of biology. You start dating a woman planning a long-term relationship. Every month right before her period starts, she gets extremely cranky like all menstruating women. However, she tells you that she has a rare medical condition called Pre-Menstrual Dysphoric Disorder or PMDD, which is the extreme form of PMS. You have already heard all about women getting agitated during their PMS, so you think that it is just the same. However, in time things get real stressful. Every month during those days, she would turn into a completely different person. And one time, she gets so agitated that she bursts out – you are the worst decision of my life. Naturally, it feels beyond acceptable to you. You are a human after all.

You cannot ignore such behavior any more. You start perceiving every single insulting word from her mouth to be true. It seems that it is what she really feels. You start getting upset beyond tolerance. And after several of such intense insults from her during those days, you realize that you don't deserve such nonsense. You have no practical idea of what PMDD really is, so you perceive the insulting and violent behavior of your woman to be extremely inappropriate. So, one day you simply go ahead and tell her – you are nothing but a psychopathic maniac who just likes to hurt people. I think it's time we ended things. Here, due to the lack of deeper understanding of what PMDD really is, your lay brain makes a decision based on your limited perception and needs, that you need to end the relationship.

CONTEXT 2

Now let's run the same experiment in a different context. Imagine yourself to be a person with a hobby of reading a lot of Science books, especially those connected to the mind. You like to learn new things. Now, you get into the same situation and the same circumstances as mentioned earlier. But, here when your girlfriend tells you about her condition after the first month of outburst in your relationship, you get really curious. Previously due to your curiosity you have already learnt about the basic biology behind PMS and how it affects the female psychology. So, hearing about PMDD, you don't only feel responsible but also very intrigued to learn about it. You feel the urge to know how can such a cheerful person turn into a completely different human being, almost like a beast?

And as you start reading, everything begins to make sense. The first thing you realize is that, PMDD is nothing like the common PMS that almost every girl faces. It is the extremely violent form of PMS, which is very rare. Due to the intense hormonal storms of PMDD inside a woman's head, her cognitive reality changes drastically during the pre-menstrual days. You start to realize what your woman has to go through every month, due to her condition. A man can never even imagine in his wildest dreams how such storm feels like.

PMDD leads to the worst of hormonal mood swings. Every month during these days she turns into a completely different person filled with hopelessness and gloom. As soon as the tides change she comes back to her real cheerful self. It is this condition which makes her say the things she would never say in a lucid mental state.

You begin to understand that for most women with PMS the hormonal changes are manageable, and they are able to somehow keep their agitation to themselves. But for your special lady, the story is different and quite unmanageable. Most weeks of the month she is brainy, creative, enthusiastic, cheerful and optimistic, but a mere shift in the hormonal flood on certain days makes her absolutely hopeless about the future, about herself, about your relationship and basically about everything that she can think of. On those days her inner instability forces her to hate herself as well as get irritated at every single action you take. And the most fascinating thing about her mental state during that time is that the hopelessness caused by hormonal imbalances feels so damn real to her that she literally perceives it as the everlasting reality of her life. The utter hormonal turbulence completely transforms her cognitive reality from a cheerful one to a gloomy one. It constructs an altered state of consciousness, in which she becomes a different personality filled with nothing but hatred and rage.

She becomes absolutely blind to all the cheerful moments of her life. And she gets so restless that she explodes with insulting words towards you. Over time, you learn that the best to do in this situation is to do nothing and just be there with her. And every time she gets cranky, you simply learn to remain patient and unaffected by her words. Every month, once the hormonal storm wears off, she comes back to her original sunny state. In time, you grow more attachment for her, and she even becomes fonder of you, because you are always there for her, even when she is mad as hell. Thus, you don't ever feel to leave her, rather together you stay forever and beyond.

ANALYSIS

In both contexts, you had two available options to choose from – leave or stay. Yet, you made totally opposite decisions in exactly the same circumstances. The only thing that was different is your understanding and experience.

In the first context, you were a layman with a general view of the world. You perceived everything in a generalized manner, with no further need of your own to explore and have deeper understanding of a phenomenon. Hence, when it came to decide whether to leave or to stay in the relationship, your brain made the decision based on your generalized understanding of everything, and you willfully preferred to leave your woman in the pursuit of a better prize, with less crankiness.

In the second context, you had a better grip over natural phenomena. Moreover, you had the curiosity to understand things, in a better way than the general public. And your understanding allowed you to try seeing the world from your woman's perspective. And the more you tried, the better you became at being next to her when she needed you the most and hated you at the same time. You got experienced at it.

Naturally, the thought of leaving her, never occurred in your mind. And even if it did, you brushed off as the spur of the moment. Because your PFC already had sufficient data on the situation to analyze and come up with a positive outcome. Your experience here served as the very foundation, of your willful support towards your woman.

- *What is Mind?*

Hence you see, it is neither love nor care that keeps a relationship alive, rather it is understanding. In fact, true love is 20 percent care and 80 percent understanding. Understanding is the key to a healthy and happy relationship. It is the key to a healthy and happy marriage. It is the most effective tool to deal with the incompatibilities between two partners. And compatibility doesn't determine the fate of a marriage, how you deal with the incompatibilities, does.

In the path of romantic love, one of the most elementary qualities is to pick up emotional cues. You have to know whenever your partner is feeling blue, even if he or she is not expressing anything. Sounds like a lot of magical effort right! But actually, it's no effort at all. Again, we must thank our brain, that it practically has gifted us with the ability to read the mind of our partner. Whether you call it "gut-feeling" or "intuition", by all means it's technically mind-reading. And biologically speaking, women are better at this than men. There is a fascinating interplay of brain circuits behind your gut-feeling. Gut-feelings are not just free-floating emotional states but actual physical sensations that convey meaning to certain areas in the brain. And studies have shown that the areas of the brain that are involved in gut-feelings are larger and more sensitive in the female brain than the male brain.

At first a woman begins receiving emotional signals from another person's facial expressions, hand gestures, body postures and breathing rates through firing of the brain cells called mirror neurons. There is no mysticism involved in it. It's just beautiful biological design.

The marvelous nerve cells of the Mirror Neuron System have literally shaped our civilization in terms of our innate tendency to help others. These tiny wonders in our brain, make us aware of what it's like to be human. They are also the reason why you start yawning or giggling merely by watching another person do the same. They play the key role in a child's brain, while he or she is learning the mother-tongue along with other cultural and sociological norms and tactics.

And as for adults, mirror neurons are the cells that significantly contribute in the process of learning new skills. In the 1980s and 1990s, a few researchers Giacomo Rizzolatti, Giuseppe Di Pellegrino, Luciano Fadiga, Leonardo Fogassi, and Vittorio Gallese at the University of Parma, Italy discovered the mirror neurons in macaque monkey. The discovery was initially sent to Nature but was rejected at that time due to "lack of general interest", only to be accepted widely in a few years.

Mirror neurons were first found in various regions of the monkey brain (Macaca nemestrina and Macaca mulatta). So far, we have observed these wonderful neurons in areas like the ventral premotor cortex (vPMC), inferior parietal lobe (IPL), primary motor cortex and dorsal premotor cortex (dPMC). Originally it was discovered that the mirror neurons (MN) discharge both when the monkey does a particular action and when it observes another individual (monkey or human) doing a similar action. The name itself implies the significant feature of MNs. This specific feature of 'mirroring' or more specifically 'imitating' has been evolutionarily crucial in shaping the modern human civilization, especially the civilization part of it.

Neurophysiological experiments demonstrate that when humans observe an action done by another individual, their motor cortex becomes active even without the presence of any motor activity. On this matter, the first evidence was provided in the 1950s by Gastaut and his coworkers. They recorded significant changes (desynchronization) in an EEG rhythm (the mu rhythm) of humans both during active movements of studied subjects and when the subjects observed actions done by others.

Later many other researchers replicated the experiment and confirmed the results. The desynchronization while observing an action carried out by others includes rhythms originating from the cortex inside the central sulcus. Transcranial magnetic stimulation (TMS) studies provide us even more direct evidence to the existence of mirroring properties in the motor system of humans.

TMS is a non-invasive technique for electrical stimulation of the nervous system. When TMS is applied to the motor cortex, at appropriate stimulation intensity, motor-evoked potentials (MEPs) can be recorded from contralateral extremity muscles. By modulating the amplitude of the MEPs through behavioral stimulation, it is possible to assess the significant effects of various experimental conditions. This way we can study the mirror neuron system in humans.

In the year 1995 Fadiga and colleagues recorded MEPs, elicited by stimulation of the left motor cortex, from the right hand and arm muscles in volunteers required to observe an experimenter grasping objects (transitive hand actions) or performing meaningless arm gestures (intransitive arm movements). The results showed that the observation of both transitive and intransitive actions made a huge impact over the MEPs and increased the recorded MEPs. The increase concerned selectively those muscles that the participants use for carrying out the exact observed actions. Amplification of the MEPs while observing actions done by the others may result from the activation of the primary motor cortex owing to mirror activity of the premotor areas.

Later in the year 2000 another study by Strafella & Paus came up with support for this cortical hypothesis. By using a double-pulse TMS technique, they demonstrated that the duration of intracortical recurrent inhibition, occurring during the observation of an action, closely corresponds to that occurring during the execution of that specific action.

Now the question was - "does the observation of actions done by others influence the spinal cord excitability?" In 2001 Baldissera and colleagues investigated the issue and discovered that there is an inhibitory mechanism in the spinal cord that prevents the execution of an observed action and leaves the motor cortex free to react to that action without the risk of any kind of movement generation.

Later many other neuroscientists showed that the motor cortical excitability faithfully follows the grasping movement phases of the observed action, or to say simply, your motor cortex area of the brain lights up whenever you see another person carrying out an action as well as when you carry it out yourself.

In conclusion, studies reveal that a mirror-neuron system exists in humans and that it possesses important properties not observed in monkeys. Intransitive meaningless movements produce mirror neuron system activation in humans but not in monkeys. These properties of the human mirror neuron system play an important role in determining the humans' capacity to imitate others' action as well as empathizing with them.

The Mirror Neuron System has vast impact over a person's social and behavioral skills throughout the lifetime. It allows us to be human and understand another human being and even other species for that matter. When you see a person get beaten up in the park, you suddenly start to feel his agony. The same happens when you see a street dog getting hurt. Humans are biologically designed to truly understand another creature's pain, happiness and desires, as if it is our own pain, happiness and desires. Feeling another person's emotions is thus one of the greatest boons of Mother Nature to us.

Brain-scan studies have shown that the simple act of observing another person in a particular emotional state can automatically trigger similar brain region activity in the observer by the grace of the Mirror Neuron System (MNS), this is what we call "emotional empathy". And females are especially good at this kind of emotional mirroring. After the mirror neurons play their part, the body sends a message to the insula and anterior cingulate cortex. The insula is an area in a classic part of the brain where gut feelings are first processed. The anterior cingulate cortex, which is larger and more easily activated in females, is a critical area for anticipating, judging, controlling, and integrating negative emotions. A woman's pulse rate suddenly bumps up, a feeling of tension felt in her belly and the brain interprets it as an intense emotion.

So, being able to guess what another person is thinking or feeling is technically very much biological. And overall, between the male and female, the female brain is efficient at assessing the thoughts, beliefs, and intentions of others, based on the smallest hints more quickly than the male brain. Such unique feature in the female brain is yet another product of evolutionary practice, as throughout evolution the women had to be very receptive of the facial expressions of their children, in order to ensure their well-being.

Now let's investigate the underlying neurobiology of this glorious fusion of mental elements, called Love. In the very early days of a relationship it is not really love, what we feel, rather it is a sensation of attraction which is subconsciously driven by libido. Love begins with this stage of primitive lust and attraction. The bodily characteristics of a person, poke the level of sex hormones (testosterone and estrogen) and pheromones. Lust is initiated at this stage through the physical attraction and flirting. This is an evolutionary behavior of humankind that biologically enables a human to find a healthy, fertile and suitable mate.

Following the cue of lust, the major attraction symptoms kick in, which are usually known as the symptoms of love, such as sweaty palms, tremors in the whole body, restlessness, loss of appetite and sleep, thumping heart, butterflies in the stomach etc. Such symptoms occur because the body is flooded with neurochemicals like Dopamine, Norepinephrine, and Phenylethylamine (PEA). It is only when this euphoria wears off, that the ultimate and deepest stage of love prevails that is the attachment phenomenon. And the chemicals that make this possible are Oxytocin, Vasopressin and Endorphins. As time goes by, the crazy love sensation diminishes and the feeling of closeness and attachment grows and thereafter prevails till the last breath of life.

Research has shown that due to the primitive programming of lust and attraction it takes the male brain only one fifth of a second to classify a woman as sexually hot or not. The unconscious mind reaches to the conclusion long before a man's conscious mind engages in the process.

For men and women, the initial calculations about romance are totally unconscious, and they are very different. Men are chasers and women are choosers. It's our inheritance from our primitive ancestors who learnt over millions of years, how to propagate their genes.

Darwin noted, males of all species are made for wooing females, and females typically choose among their suitors. This is the brain architecture of love, engineered by the reproductive winners in evolution. Even the shapes, faces, smells, and ages of the mates we choose are influenced by patterns set ages ago.

Falling in love is one of the most irrational behaviors or brain states imaginable for both men and women. The brain becomes "illogical" in the throes of new romance. If we could travel along a person's brain circuits as he or she is falling in love, we'd begin in an area deep at the center of the brain called the ventral tegmental area (VTA). We'd see the cells in this area rapidly producing dopamine.

Dopamine is the brain's feel-good neurotransmitter for motivation and reward. As the brain gets filled with dopamine, the person starts to feel a pleasant buzz. The flood of dopamine stimulates the nucleus accumbens (NAc), the brain region involved in the feeling of pleasure and reward, or simply the brain's reward center.

In a male brain, we'd see the dopamine being mixed with testosterone and vasopressin, while in a female brain, it gets mixed with estrogen and oxytocin. The fusion of dopamine with these other hormones makes an addictive impact over the person, leaving both the male and female exhilarated and head over heels in love.

And the last stand of this mad love is the caudate nucleus (CN), the area for memorizing the look and identity of whoever is giving pleasure. Here we'd see all the minuscule details about the woman or the man being indelibly chiseled into the permanent memory. At this point your beloved one becomes literally unforgettable. Once the train of love has made these three stops at the VTA, NAc and CN, we'd see the brain's lust and love circuits merge together as they focus only on the beloved one.

The brain circuits for passionately being in love or the so-called infatuation-love share brain circuits with states of obsession, mania, intoxication, thirst, and hunger. Also, as I mentioned earlier the brain circuits that are activated when we are in love match those of the drug addict desperately craving for the next fix.

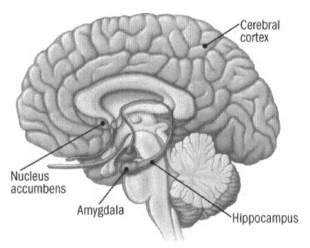

Figure 4.1 Nucleus accumbens, Amygdala, Hippocampus and Cortex

The amygdala (fear-alert system) and the prefrontal cortex (judgment and critical thinking system) are turned way down when the love circuits are running at their full potential. This is why we become literally blind to the shortcomings of our dearly beloved. The same thing happens when people take Ecstasy. So romantic love is a natural way of getting high. The classic symptoms of early love are also similar to the initial effects of drugs such as cocaine, heroin and morphine. Narcotics trigger the brain's reward circuit, causing effects similar to romance. Hence the well-known phrase "addicted to love" is scientifically quite literal and accurate.

Studies have shown that this early ecstatic stage of romantic love lasts for around six to eight months. During this stage break-up can be catastrophic leading to withdrawal like symptoms, as the body keeps hankering for the sensation of euphoria connected to the person. These early months of a relationship, romantically involved partners literally crave for each other and feel undeniably dependent on each other. This is such an extreme state that the partner's well-being becomes more important than one's own.

After the euphoria of the mad love phase wears off, the powerful emotional bond between two romantically involved partners starts to build up. The lessons of relationship and pair-bonding that our primordial ancestors learnt are deeply encoded in our modern brains as neurological circuits of love. They are present from the moment we're born and activated at puberty by the cocktail of neurochemicals. It's an elegant synchronized system.

At first our brain weighs a potential partner, and if the person fits our ancestral wish-list, we get a spike in the release of chemicals that makes us dizzy with a rush of unavoidable infatuation. It's the first step down the road that leads to pair-bonding. And it is this bond, that defines the true merit of a relationship. Moreover, it is the truest form of love that you can experience in a relationship.

The mirror neurons of a man allow him to briefly feel the same emotional pain he sees in his woman's face. Next, the temporo-parietal junction activates his brain's analytical circuits to search his entire brain for solutions. This is called "cognitive empathy". The male brain is able to use the temporo-parietal junction starting in late childhood, and after puberty a man's reproductive hormones reinforces the preference for it. Researchers have found that the temporo-parietal junction keeps a firm boundary between emotions of the "self" and the "other". This prevents men's thought processes from being infected by other people's emotional weakness, which strengthens their ability to cognitively and analytically find a solution without being vulnerable.

Many women in relationship often complain that their men are blind to the emotional signals they send. That's not actually their fault. While the female brain is a high-performance emotion engine, the male brain is not so skilled at reading facial expressions and emotional innuendoes like signs of despair and hopelessness. Men pick up the subtle signs of sadness in a female face only 40 percent of the time, whereas women can pick up these signs 90 percent of the time. The only way to penetrate their shell of logical thinking, is to burst into tears. It's only when men actually see tears, they realize, that something's wrong. Perhaps that's why women have evolved to cry four times more easily than men by displaying an unambiguous sign of suffering that men can't ignore. Tears in a woman's eyes literally force a man to feel intense pain. A man feels absolutely powerless when he sees his woman in pain. And then the inevitable happens, that is an automatic comforting hug from the man.

However, a relationship doesn't get ruined because of such a vivid biological difference in the brain circuits between men and women. Rather it's about patience. In a typical scenario, a male brain needs to go through a longer process to interpret emotional meaning. Most men just don't bother to take the time to figure out the emotion, and they become impatient.

A man may not be so skilled at picking up emotional signals, all he needs to maintain a healthy relationship is to practice the skill of patience. Over time, he'd learn to recognize when his special lady needs a good cry and then he could simply hold her in his arms and be with her until she's done.

One of the beautiful innate qualities of a woman is to be there with her man (or woman) during emotionally difficult times, which is why she is often baffled by her partner's inability to put up with her sadness or despair. Women are neurologically wired to respond to the distress of other people. So when men say "women blow things out of proportion", what they don't realize is that the male brain is a high-performance logicality machine, while on the other hand the woman's brain is neurologically programmed by Mother Nature to be more sensitive to emotional distress.

Studies have also shown that the connections between the emotion centers in women are more active and extensive than men. In another study, at Stanford University, volunteers looked at emotional images while having their brains scanned. Nine different brain areas lit up in women, while in men only two lit up. No wonder, a woman always sticks around when her man is hurt or disturbed and would do everything in her capacity to make him feel comfortable. While on the contrary men tend to avoid contact with emotionally distressed people. Men tend to process their troubles alone and expect women would do the same, which is just the opposite of what women expect.

It is all determined by the neurons inside your head. The neurons create who you are. They create your passions. They create your ambitions. They create your unique identity, based on experiences. In fact, when you say "I", it is actually your neurons, that are collectively expressing their functional existence. To put it simply, your neurons create, shape and reshape your "soul" throughout your lifetime and it dies when your brain stops functioning. If we take away a portion of the neural network inside your brain, a significant portion of your individual identity would suddenly disappear, which would radically alter your entire personality – it would alter your soul.

In a relationship, your brain constructs distinct neuronal connections for you partner. Over time, these connections become intertwined with the connections that construct your own identity. This way a significant portion of a person's identity gets imprinted into the neural network of his or her partner's brain. Thus, two married partners do not just live with each other, they live in each other, neurologically speaking. And studies have revealed that people who stay married live around four years longer than people who don't.

A good marriage, where both partners are exclusively committed to each other, keeps them healthier both physiologically and psychologically, by directly influencing the nervous system and immune system. In contrast, a divorce can depress the immune system's healthy functioning. And this depression in the system's ability to fight foreign invaders leaves a divorced individual open to more infectious diseases. Not only do happily married people avoid this drop in immune function, but their immune systems keep getting an extra boost by staying married. Happily married couples have a far lower rate of maladies. They also tend to be more health-conscious than others.

In a study, where researchers tested the immune system responses of fifty couples who stayed overnight in the Love Lab, they found a striking difference between those who were very satisfied with their marriages and those whose emotional response to each other was neutral or who were unhappy. The scientists used blood samples from each subject to test the response of the white blood cells, which are the immune system's major defense weapons. In general, happily married men and women showed a greater proliferation of these white blood cells when exposed to foreign invaders than did the other subjects.

They also tested the effectiveness of other immune system warriors - the natural killer cells, which, true to their name, destroy body cells that have been damaged or altered (such as infected or cancerous ones) and are known to limit the growth of tumor cells. Again, subjects who were satisfied with their marriage had more effective natural killer cells than did the others. If the fitness buffs spent just 10 percent of their weekly workout time, working on their marriage instead of their bodies, they would get three times the health benefits they get from running on the treadmill!

Hence, make a little effort to work on your marriage, and you will be healthier than usual. Remember a key principle of a healthy marriage, my friend, -

try to respond to your partner instead of reacting.

You do not always have to win. You do not always need to prove your point. Marriage is not a competition. Marriage is completion of two souls. It is the unification of two minds. Remember, there is no rush in marriage. There is no destination in marriage. It is the journey that matters.

5.
Civilized & Wise

Polygamy is a luxury of the cave-people, and monogamy is an existential responsibility of the civilized society. Remember, the more we cleanse the civilization of all impurities and primitiveness, the more we will become civilized. The more we humanize the society, the more we will become humans. Hanging on to our primitive urges only deteriorates us as humans. Humans are those who can recognize their internal primitive evil and have a healthy control over it. Call it social conduct – call it social construct – call it whatever you want. But our civilized control over our innate evil is what makes us civilized – it is what makes us a wise species.

Civilized are not those who never make mistakes – civilized are those who learn from their mistakes instead of trying to justify them. Mistakes are a quintessential part of human civilization. We can progress only when we make mistakes. Without mistakes there is no progress. Our mistakes rewire our brain and open up new gateways of perception. And these gateways take us closer to becoming a real wise species.

In a civilized world, after making a mistake, if a person is truly remorseful and prepared to learn from it, then that person truly deserves to be forgiven by the people who are affected by that mistake. But if an individual says, "sorry honey, but I have natural desires for other people, so I will sleep with them", then such an individual is a creature with a broken mind, that needs to be fixed by a psychiatrist, because this kind of behavior is a threat to the progress and wellbeing of humanity. Making mistakes, no matter how disgraceful they are, is very much human, but advocating for those mistakes as signs of progressive thinking is the work of uncivilized inferior creatures, unfit to be called humans. Just because some dogs look like humans, does not make they are humans.

Remember this, cheating is an innate evolutionarily programmed desire, especially in men, but it is not a desire that cannot be controlled. Mark you, there is a difference between what you want, and what you need.

Our mind has evolved in such a way that new wants keep appearing in it relentlessly. But do not confuse them with needs. Needs are necessity, but wants are luxury. And it is when you learn to convince yourself, that just because you want something does not mean you need it, that you would become a truly civilized, rational and wise human being. Remember, the fate of the human civilization is predicated on the rational decision-making capacities of the humans. It is predicated on you. So, let's try to perceive how exactly we humans make a rational and civilized decision or choice.

CELLULAR MECHANISM OF DECISION-MAKING

Given a situation, where you need to make a decision, the prefrontal cortex (PFC) of your brain, first analyzes all the options available to you while accessing the correlated implicit and explicit memory of your past experiences. Then in context of a set of needs and your personal history, the PFC potentiates the neural pathway for the execution of the most preferable among all the possible options.

Various regions of the prefrontal cortex are involved in distinctive cognitive and behavioral operations. And the regions that are specifically involved in various aspects of decision-making are - ventromedial prefrontal cortex (vmPFC), dorsolateral prefrontal cortex (dlPFC) and orbitofrontal cortex (OFC).

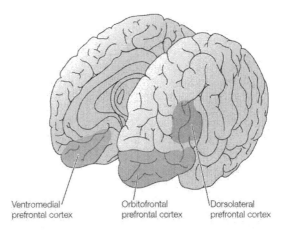

Ventromedial prefrontal cortex   Orbitofrontal prefrontal cortex   Dorsolateral prefrontal cortex

Figure 5.1 Prefrontal regions involved in decision-making

The vmPFC is crucial for your freedom of will to make a decision. Patients with bilateral lesions in the vmPFC develop severe impairment in personal and social decision-making, even though most other intellectual mental abilities remain intact. Damage to this region (especially in the right hemisphere) also leads to mental deficit in detecting irony, sarcasm and deception. People with damaged vmPFC are prone to be easily influenced by misleading advertising, due to their lack of doubt and skepticism.

The ventromedial prefrontal cortex is connected to and receives input from the ventral tegmental area, amygdala, the temporal lobe, the olfactory system, and the dorsomedial thalamus. It, in turn, sends signals to many different brain regions including, the temporal lobe, the amygdala, the lateral hypothalamus, the hippocampal formation, the cingulate cortex, and certain other regions of the prefrontal cortex. This huge network of connections affords the vmPFC the ability to receive and monitor large amounts of sensory data and thereafter influence your decision-making ability.

Emotions are a significant part of our mental lives. And vmPFC plays a key role in regulating emotions and inhibiting them if necessary, by influencing the limbic system, particularly the amygdala. The neural circuitry of the vmPFC is the birthplace of the moral nature of your behaviors and beliefs. Hence, malfunction in this region of your brain, cripples the very element of your mental morality. Without the healthy activity of the vmPFC individuals endorse actions of self-preservation that often break moral values associated with the term human, and inflict harm to others. And the most glaring instance of such vmPFC deficit can be seen in the phenomenon of religious terrorism, or more commonly jihad.

On the other hand, another crucial brain region involved in decision-making is dorsolateral prefrontal cortex (dlPFC). It manages various cognitive functions of the mind, such as working memory, cognitive flexibility, and planning. And when it comes to decision-making, dlPFC carries out all the risky stuff. When given several options to choose from, the dlPFC evokes the mental preference towards the most reasonable option while suppressing temptation in order to maximize personal gain. It gives birth to the ability of self-control in a certain situation for a better outcome. Unlike the vmPFC which makes decisions based upon moral values, healthy activity in the dlPFC facilitates self-preservation. In particular, it plays three distinct roles in your mental life:

1. provides cognitive control to override predominant social-emotional responses elicited by the dilemmas,

2. facilitates abstract reasoning, such as, cost-benefit analyses, and

3. generates self-centered and other-aversive emotions such as, anger, frustration, or moral disgust.

Also, quite fascinatingly, several studies have shown that, increased activity of the dlPFC is often associated with psychopathic traits.

Thus, both the vmPFC and dlPFC are intertwined at a functional level along with another prefrontal region called the orbitofrontal cortex, when it comes to make a decision. Increased activity of the dlPFC without the correlated functions of the vmPFC leads to apparently inhuman and antisocial traits of psychopathy. On the other hand, without the healthy activity of the dlPFC, you would probably start to show altruistic attitude. Thus, in order to sustain a healthy life, dlPFC and vmPFC keep each other in check. In fact, when the both are working in proper harmony, you'd have excellent self-control as well as fantastically effective moral values, that would ultimately enrich your mental life. In simple terms, moral values are encoded in your vmPFC, and effective selfishness is encoded in your dlPFC. And you need both, in order to survive.

Orbitofrontal cortex also plays a significant role in decision-making. It enables you to anticipate the possible reward or punishment in a certain situation. It signals the expected rewards/punishments of an action given the particular details of a situation. In doing this, the brain is capable of comparing the expected reward/punishment with the actual delivery of reward/punishment, thus, making the OFC critical for adaptive learning. Thus, OFC plays the part in your mental life, where it analyses the potential emotional outcome of a certain decision in a specific situation.

- *What is Mind?*

This way, every single decision of your life is predicated on the healthy functioning of the prefrontal cortex. Even a slight malfunction in a tiny chunk of neuron anywhere in the PFC would lead to the mental deficit in your logical decision-making. The healthier your PFC, the better you are at making the best decisions and choices in your life for both the self and the society.

Remember my friend, uncontrolled alcohol, uncontrolled casual sex and mindless indoctrination are not signs of progress, they are signs of drowning into the abyss of mental and physical degradation. If you want to be drunk, become drunk with an idea. If you want pleasure, have pleasure from the pursuit of your passion. If you want to be indoctrinated, then be so by the natural law of humanism.

Progress begins with the uplift of the soul. Progress begins when you liberate your mind from the shackles of your ingrained tendencies of authoritarianism – the tendencies of greed – the tendencies of hatred, rage and lust. Remember my friend, there is both good and evil inside you. Do not let the evil dictate your life. Do not let the evil dictate your society. Do not let the evil be the master of our fate. Bring out the good from within and spread it among the masses.

It is you who can choose the good over the evil, with your faculties of reasoning, love and conscience. It is you my friend, who decides, what happens to your relationship. It is you, my friend, who decides what happens to your life. It is you, my friend, who decides what happens to your society. I say again, do not let the evil become our masters, but make the good reign upon the world.

What is the point of having a civilization, if we do not practice being civilized! What is the point of having an intellect, if we use it for the same purposes that we used to use our primitiveness for, in the wild! What is the point of being humans, if our actions scream with more bestiality than humanity! Humanity is not a word my friend. It is a symbol – a symbol of hope – a symbol of wisdom – yet this very symbol has become disgraced by our faults and deluded justification of mistakes. Arise, my friend – the world is wailing for kindness – it is wailing for compassion – it is wailing for love. Rise to become human again, my friend. Become the human that we see no longer in our society.

Become the human that has gone extinct from the planet. Become the human, that talks humans, acts humans and lives human.

A human is the one, who would give up a thousand Cleopatras to be with the person he or she loves. A human is the one, who would give up his or her life to save a child from being crushed by a truck. A human is the one, who would choose reasoning and compassion over bigotry. A human is the one, who would see all other humans as equal, regardless of what his or her scripture or society says. Are you the human, my friend? Are you?

Today is the day, that you need to make a decision – a decision on whether you will keep on ignoring all the hatred, greed and sectarianism in your society, or choose to speak up against such primitive evil. The fate of the whole world lies on your decision. Your decision shall determine whether your children shall live in a petty so-called civilized society devoid of all peace and goodness, or they shall live in a world of love, peace and wellbeing. You need to decide my friend. You need to decide today. Goodness or Evil? Racism or Humanism? Promiscuity or Commitment? Sexism or Egalitarianism? Fundamentalism or Reasoning?

You can choose to ignore these questions today, but by doing so, you are only ensuring a dark and evil future for you children. If you don't decide today, your children will grow up and they will be given the same choices, except they will have to make their decision in much worse circumstances than you. I urge to you – do not let that happen my friend. Do something, while you still can, otherwise in your deathbed you will regret that you have given everything to your children that they wanted, except the one thing that they really needed, that is a society of peace, conscience and harmony.

You may be thinking, "what can I possibly do, alone". Let me tell you, you are not alone. For once, awaken the conscientious human within you and bring it out. Then you will see, many more shall follow your footsteps. They are only waiting for someone to take the first step. Be that someone my friend. Be that person whose footsteps shall become the first conscientious footsteps of the human civilization towards becoming real humans. You are not a person. You are a ray of hope – the ray that can enlighten the darkest corners of your society. You have all the brightness within you. All you need to do, is to recognize that brightness and take it out. Bring that internal light out and caste it upon the world. And you shall visualize the dawn of the real human civilization.

BIBLIOGRAPHY

Acevedo BP, Aron A, Fisher HE & Brown LL (2011). Neural correlates of long-term intense romantic love. Social Cognitive and Affective Neuroscience, published online January 5 2011 doi:10.1093/scan/nsq092.

Aron A (2006). Relationship neuroscience: Advancing the social psychology of close relationships using functional neuroimaging. In PAM Van Lange (Ed) Bridging social psychology: Benefits of transdisciplinary approaches, Lawrence Erlbaum Associates Publishers Mahwah NJ.

Aron A (2010). Behavior the brain and the social psychology of close relationships. In CR Agnew, DE Carlston, WG Graziano & JR Kelly (Eds) Then a miracle occurs: Focusing on behavior in social psychological theory and research, Oxford University Press New York.

Aron A, Fisher H, Mashek DJ, Strong G, Li H & Brown LL (2005). Reward motivation and emotion systems associated with early-stage intense romantic love. Journal of Neurophysiology 94.

Aron AP & Aron EN (1986). Love as the expansion of self: Understanding attraction and satisfaction. Hemisphere, New York.

Aron AP & Aron EN (1991). Love and sexuality. In K McKinney & S Sprecher (Eds.) Sexuality in close relationship. Lawrence Erlbaum Associates, Hillsdale, NJ.

Abbot, David H. 1993 Social Conflict and Reproductive Success in Marmoset and Tamarin Monkeys. In Primate Social Conflict. B. Mason and S. Mendoza, eds. Pp. 331-372. Albany; State University of New York Press.

Ahsan, Farid 1995 Fighting between Two Females for a Male in the

Hoolock Gibbon. International Journal of Primatology 16(5):731-737.

Aiello, L. C, and R. I. M. Dunbar 1993 Neocortex Size, Group Size, and the Evolution of Language. Current Anthropology 34(2): 184-193.

Alterman, L., G. A. Doyle, and M. K. Izard, eds. 1995 Creatures of the Dark: The Nocturnal Prosimians. New York: Plenum Press.

Anzenberger, Gustl 1988 The Pairbond in the Titi Monkey (Callicebus moloch): Intrinsic versus Extrinsic Contributions of the Pairmates. Folia Primatologica 50:188-203.

1992 Monogamous Social Systems and Paternity in Primates. In Paternity in Primates: Genetic Tests and Theories. R. D. Martin, A. F. Dixson, and E. J. Wicklings, eds. Pp. 203-224. Basel: Karger.

Aquino, R., and F. Encarnacion 1986 Population Structure of Aotus nancymai (Cebidae: Primates) in Peruvian Amazon Lowland Rainforest. American Journal of Primatology 11:1-7.

Aquino, R., P. Puertas, and F. Encarnacion 1990 Supplemental Notes on Population Parameters of Northeastern Peruvian Night Monkeys, Genus Aotus (Cebidae). American Journal of Primatology 21:215-221.

A. (2014). Psychosocial impact of polygamy in the Middle East. New York: Springer.

Al-Krenawi, A., & Graham, J. R. (2006). A comparison of family functioning, life and marital satisfaction, and mental health of women in polygamous and monogamous marriages. International Journal of Social Psychiatry, 52(1), 5-17.

Al-Krenwai, A., Graham, J., AL-Krenwai, S. (1997). Social work practice with polygamous families. Child and Adolescent Social Work Journal, 14(6), 4, 445-458.

Al-Krenawi, A., Graham, J. R., & Ben-Shimol-Jacobsen, S. (2006). Attitudes toward and reasons for polygamy differentiated by gender and age among Bedouin-Arab of the Negev. International Journal of Mental Health, 35(1),46-61. 19

Al-Krenawi, A., Graham, J., Slonim-Nevo, V. (2002). Mental health aspects of Arab-Israeli adolescents from polygamous versus monogamous families. Journal of Social Psychology, 142(4) 446-460.

Al-Krenawi, A., & Lightman, E. S. (2000). Learning achievement, social adjustment, and family conflict among Bedouin-Arab children from polygamous and monogamous families. Journal of Social Psychology,140(3), 345-355.

Al-Krenawi, A., Slonim-Nevo, V., & Graham, J. R. (2006). Polygyny and its impact on the psychological well-being of husbands. Journal of Comparative Family Studies, 3(45), 173-189.

Al-Krenawi, A., Slonim-Nevo, V. (2008). Psychosocial and familial functioning of children from polygamous and monogamous families. Journal of Social Psychology, 148(2), 745-764.

Al-Shamsi, M., & Fulcher, L. (2005). The impact of polygamy on United Arab Emirates first wives and their children. International Journal of Child & Family Welfare, (1), 46-55.

Bartels A & Zeki S (2000). The neural basis of romantic love. Neuroreport: For Rapid Communication of Neuroscience Research 11.

Bartels A & Zeki S (2004). The neural correlates of maternal and romantic love. Neuroimage 21.

Basson R (2000). The female sexual response: A different model. Journal of Sex & Marital Therapy 26, 51-65.

Basson R (2002). Women's sexual desire: Disordered or misunderstood? Journal of Sex & Marital Therapy 28.

Basson R, Wierman ME, van Lankveld J & Brotto L (2010). Summary of the recommendations on sexual dysfunctions in women. Journal of Sexual Medicine 7.

Baumeister RF (2000). Gender differences in erotic plasticity: The female sex drive as socially flexible and responsive. Psychological Bulletin 126.

Beauregard M, Courtemanche J, Paquette V & St-Pierre EL (2009). The neural basis of unconditional love. Psychiatry Research: Neuroimaging 172.

Bianchi-Demicheli F, Grafton ST & Ortigue S (2006). The power of love on the human brain. Social Neuroscience 1.

Bocher M, Chisin R, Parag Y, Freedman N, Meir Weil Y, Lester H et al. (2001). Cerebral activation associated with sexual arousal in response to a pornographic clip: A 15O-H2O PET study in heterosexual men. Neuroimage 14.

Brotto LA, Bitzer J, Laan E, Leiblum SR & Luria M (2010). Women's sexual desire and arousal disorders. Journal of Sexual Medicine 7.

Bamgbade, E. O., & Saloviita, T. (2014). School Performance of Children From Monogamous and Polygamous Families in Nigeria. Journal of Black Studies, 45(7), 620-634.

Bewley, A. and Bewley, A. (1999). The noble Qur'an. A new rendering of its meaning in English. Dubai: Bookwork.

Booth, A., Papaioannou, D., & Sutton, A. (2012). Systematic approaches to a successful literature review. London: Sage.

Borkenau, P., Mauer, N., Riemann, R., Spinath, F. M., & Angleitner, A. (2004). Thin slices of behavior as cues to personality and intelligence. Journal of Personality and Social Psychology, 86(4), 599–614.

Buss, D. M. (1989). Sex-differences in human mate preferences—evolutionary hypothesis tested in 37 cultures. Behavioral and Brain Sciences, 12(1), 1–14.

Buss, D. M., & Schmitt, D. P. (1993). Sexual Strategies Theory: An evolutionary perspective on human mating. Psychological Review, 100 (2), 204–232.

Buunk, B. P., Dijkstra, P., Fetchenhauer, D., & Kenrick, D. T. (2002). Age and gender differences in mate selection criteria for various involvement levels. Personal Relationships, 9, 271–278.

Carter CS (1998). Neuroendocrine perspectives on social attachment and love. Psychoneuroendocrinology 23.

Carter CS & Keverne EB (2002). The neurobiology of social affiliation and pair bonding. In J Pfaff AP Arnold AE Etgen & SE Fahrbach (Eds) Hormones brain and behavior, vol. 1. Academic Press, New York.

Campbell A. The limbic system and emotion in relation to acupuncture. Acupuncture in Medicine.1999.

Cowan CP, Cowan PA. When Partners Become Parents: The Big Life Change for Couples. New York: Basic Books; 1992.

Chivers ML & Bailey JM (2005). A sex difference in features that elicit genital response. Biological Psychology 70.

Chivers ML, Rieger G, Latty E & Bailey JM (2004). A sex difference in the specificity of sexual arousal. Psychological Science 15.

Chivers ML Seto MC & Blanchard R (2007). Gender and sexual orientation differences in sexual response to sexual activities versus gender of actors in sexual films. Journal of Personality and Social Psychology 93.

Cook, R. "Mirror neurons: From origin to function" Behavioral and Brain Sciences 2014.

Cherian, Varghese I. (1994). Corporal punishment and academic achievement of Xhosa children from polygamous and monogamous families. Journal of Social Psychology, 134(3), 387-389.

Damasio, A. (1999) The Feeling of What Happens: Body, Emotion and the Making of Consciousness. London, Heinemann.

Darwin, C. (1859) On the Origin of Species by Means of Natural Selection. London, Murray.

Darwin, C. (1871) The Descent of Man and Selection in Relation to Sex. London, John Murray.

Darwin, C. (1872) The Expression of the Emotions in Man and Animals. London, John Murray; also published 1965, Chicago, University of Chicago Press.

Dawkins, M.S. (1987) Minding and mattering. In C. Blakemore and S. Greenfield (eds) Mindwaves. Oxford, Blackwell, 151-60.

Dawkins, R. (1976) The Selfish Gene. Oxford, Oxford University Press; a new edition, with additional material, was published in 1989.

Dawkins, R. (1986) The Blind Watchmaker. London, Longman.

Dasgupta, N. Mechanisms underlying the malleability of implicit prejudice and stereotypes: the role of automaticity and cognitive control. in Handbook of Stereotyping, Prejudice, and Discrimination (ed. Nelson, T.) 267–284 (Psychol. Press, 2009)

Delgado, M.R., Jou, R.L., LeDoux, J.E. & Phelps, E.A. Avoiding negative outcomes: tracking the mechanisms of avoidance learning in humans during fear conditioning. Front. Behav. Neurosci. 3, 33 (2009)

Deikman, A.J. (2000) A functional approach to mysticism. Journal of Consciousness Studies 7(11-12), 75-91.

Dennett, D.C. (1987) The Intentional Stance. Cambridge, MA, MIT Press.

Dennett, D.C. (1988) Quining qualia. In A.J. Marcel and E. Bisiach (eds) Consciousness in Contemporary Science. Oxford, Oxford University Press, 42-77.

Dennett, D.C. (1991) Consciousness Explained. Boston, MA, and London, Little, Brown and Co.

Duncan, G. J., & Brooks-Gunn, J. (2000). Family poverty, welfare reform and child development. Child Development, 71(1), 188-196.

Eapen, V., Al-Gazali, L., Bin-Othman, S., & Abou-Saleh, M. (1998). Mental health problems among schoolchildren in United Arab Emirates: Prevalence and risk factors. Journal of the American Academy of Child & Adolescent Psychiatry, 37(8), 880-886.

Elbedour, S., Onwuegbuzie, A. J., Caridine, C., & Abu-Saad, H. (2002). The effect of polygamous marital structure on behavioral, emotional, and academic adjustment in children: A comprehensive review of literature. Child and Family Psychology Review, 5(4), 555-271.

Elbedour, S., Bart, W., Hektner, J. (2000). Scholastic achievement and family marital structure: Bedouin-Arab adolescent from monogamous and polygamous families in Israel. Journal of Social Psychology, 140, 503-514.

Elbedour, S., Bart., W., Hektner., J. (2003). Intelligence and family marital structure: The case of adolescents from monogamous and polygamous families among Bedouin-Arab in Israel. Journal of Social Psychology, 143(1), 95-110.

Elbedour, S., Bart, W., Hektner, J. (2007). The relationship between monogamous/polygamous family structure and the mental health of Bedouin-Arab adolescents. Journal of Adolescence, 30, 213-230.

Elbedour, S., Hektner, J., Morad, M., Abu-Bader, S. (2003). Parent-adolescent conflict and its resolution in monogamous and polygamous Bedouin-Arab families in Southern

Israel. The Scientific World Journal, 3, 1249-1264.

Elbedour, S., Onwuegbuzie, A. J., Alatamin, M. (2003). Behavioral Problems and scholastic adjustment among Bedouin-Arab families children from polygamous and monogamous marital structures: Some developmental considerations. Genetic, Social, and General Psychology Monographs, 129(3), 213-237.

Ferretti A, Caulo M, Del Gratta C, Di Matteo R, Merla A, Montorsi F et al. (2005). Dynamics of male sexual arousal: distinct components of brain activation revealed by fMRI. Neuroimage 26

Fisher HE (1998). Lust attraction and attachment in mammalian reproduction. Human Nature 9

Fonteille V & Stoleru S. (2010). The cerebral correlates of sexual desire:

Functional neuroimaging approach. Sexologies 10.1016/j.sexol.2010.03.011.

Goodwin, R. (1999). Personal relationships across cultures. London: Routledge.

Gough, D., Oliver, S., & Thomas, J. (2012). An introduction to systematic reviews. London: Sage Publications.

Gangestad, S. W., Garver-Apgar, C. E., Simpson, J. A., & Cousins, A. J. (2007). Changes in women's mate preferences across the ovulatory cycle. Journal of Personality and Social Psychology, 92(1), 151–163.

Gangestad, S. W., & Simpson, J. A. (2000). The evolution of human mating: Trade-offs and strategic pluralism. Behavioral and Brain Sciences, 23, 573–644.

Gangestad, S. W., Simpson, J. A., Cousins, A. J., Garver-Apgar, C. E., & Christensen, P. N. (2004). Women's preferences for male behavioral displays change across the menstrual cycle. Psychological Science, 15 (3), 203–207.

Gangestad, S. W., & Thornhill, R. (1998). Menstrual cycle variation in wome's preference for the scent of symmetrical men. Proceedings of the Royal Society of London B, 262, 727–733.

Gangestad, S. W., & Thornhill, R. (2008). Human oestrus. Proceedings of the Royal Society of London B, 275(1638), 991–1000.

Geary, D. C., Vigil, J., & Bryd-Craven, J. (2004). Evolution of human mate choice. The Journal of Sex Research, 41(1), 27–42.

Gottfredson, L. S., & Deary, I. J. (2004). Intelligence predicts health and longevity, but why? Current Directions in Psychological Science, 13 (10), 1–4.

Garber, P., F. Encarnacion, L. Moya, and J. D. Pruetz 1993 Demographic and Reproductive Patterns in Moustached Tamarin Monkeys (Saguinus mystax): Implications for Reconstructing Platyrrhine Mating Systems. American Journal of Primatology 29:235-254.

Gautier, Jean-Pierre 1985 Quelques caracteristiques ecologiques du singe des marais, Alenopithecus nigrivoides Lang 1923. Revue d'Ecologie (Terre et Vie) 40:331-342.

Gautier-Hion, A., F. Bourliere, J. Gautier, and J. Kingdon, eds. 1988 A Primate Radiation: Evolutionary Biology of the African Guenons. Cambridge: Cambridge University Press.

Gautier-Hion, A., and J. P. Gautier 1978 Le singe de brazza: Une strategic originale. Zeitschrift fur Tierpsychologie 48:84-104.

Goldizen, Anne W. 1987 Tamarins and Marmosets: Communal Care of Offspring. In Primate Societies. B. B. Smuts, D. L. Cheney, R. M. Seyfarth, R. W. Wrangham, and T. T. Struhsaker, eds. Pp. 34-43. Chicago: University of Chicago Press. 1988 Tamarin and Marmoset Mating Systems: Unusual Flexibility. Tree 3(2):36-40.

Goldizen, A. W., M. Mendelson, M. van Vlaardingen, and J. Terborgh 1996 Saddle-Back Tamarin (Saguinus fuscicolis) Reproductive Strategies: Evidence from a Thirteen-Year Study of a Marked Population. American Journal of Primatology 38:57-83.

Goodhart, Charles B. 1991 Origins and Future of Human Monogamy. In Primatology Today. A. Ehara, T. Kimura, O. Takenaka, and M. Iwamoto, eds. Pp. 251-258. Amsterdam: Elsevier Science Publishers.

Gough, Katheleen E. 1959 The Nayars and the Definition of Marriage. Journal of the Royal Anthropological Institute 89:49-71.

Gowaty, Patricia A. 1996 Battles of the Sexes and Origins of Monogamy. In Partnership in Birds: The Study of Monogamy. J. Black, ed. Pp. 21-52. New York: Oxford University Press.

Gursky, Sharon L. 1995 Group Size and Composition in the Spectral Tarsier, Tarsius spectrum: Implications for Social Organization. Tropical Biodiversity 3(l):57-62.

Hamdan, S., Auerbach, J., & Apter, A. (2009). Polygamy and mental health of adolescents. European Child & Adolescent Psychiatry, 18(12), 755-760.

Hrdy, S. B. (2000). "The optimal number of fathers: Evolution, demography, and history in the shaping of female mate preferences." Ann NY Acad Sci 907

Huber, D., P. Veinante, et al. (2005). "Vasopressin and oxytocin excite distinct neuronal populations in the central amygdala." Science 308

Hultcrantz, M. (2006). "Estrogen and hearing: A summary of recent investigations." Acta Otolaryngol 126

Hamann S Herman RA Nolan CL & Wallen K (2004). Men and women differ in amygdala response to visual sexual stimuli. Nature Neuroscience 7.

Hatfield E & Sprecher S. (1986). Measuring passionate love in intimate relationships. Journal of Adolescence 9

Hatfield E. Love, Sex and Intimacy. New York: Harper Collins 1993.

Heaton JP, Adams MA. Update on central function relevant to sex: remodeling the basis of drug treatments for sex and the brain. Int J Impot Res 2003.

Heinzel A, Walter M, Schneider F, Rotte M, Matthiae C, Tempelmann C et al. (2006). Self-related processing in the sexual domain: Parametric event-related fMRI study reveals neural activity in ventral cortical midline structures. Social Neuroscience 1

Kilbride, P. L., & Kilbride, J. C. (1990). Changing family life in East Africa: women and children at risk. University Park, PA: The Penn State University Press.

Lauglin, Charles, John McManus, and Eugene d'Aquili. Brain, Symbol, and Experience. 2nd ed. New York: Columbia University Press, 1992

Lakoff, G. and M. Johnson (1999). Philosophy in the flesh. Basic Books: New York.

LeDoux, J. E. (1996). The emotional brain. New York: Simon & Schuster.

LeDoux, J.E. (1992), 'Emotion and the amygdala', in The Amygdala:

Neurobiological Aspects of Emo- tion, Memory and Mental Dysfunction, ed J.P. Aggleton (New York: Wiley-Liss).

Levin, D.T. and Simons, D.J. (1997) Failure to detect changes to attended objects in motion pictures. Psychonomic Bulletin and Review 4, 501-6.

Levine,J. (1983) Materialism and qualia: the explanatory gap. Pacific Philosophical Quarterly 64, 354-61.

Levine,J. (2001) Purple Haze: The Puzzle of Consciousness. New York, Oxford University Press. Levine, S. (1979) A Gradual Awakening. New York, Doubleday.

Levinson, B.W. (1965) States of awareness during general anaesthesia. British Journal of Anaesthesia 37, 544-6.

Lewicki, P., Czyzewska, M. and Hoffman, H. (1987) Unconscious acquisition of complex procedural knowledge. Journal of Experimental

Psychology: Learning, Memory and Cognition 13, 523-30.

Lewicki, P., Hill, T. and Bizot, E. (1988) Acquisition of procedural knowledge about a pattern of stimuli that cannot be articulated. Cognitive Psychology 20, 24-37.

Lewicki, P., Hill, T. and Czyzewska, M. (1992) Nonconscious acquisition of information. American Psychologist 47, 796-801.

McNab, Warren. (1993). "Masturbation: The Neglected Topic in Sexuality Education." Family Life Education, 12(2) : 10-15.

Michael, Robert T, John H. Gagnon, Edward O. Laumann, & Gina Kolata. (1994). Sex In America: A Definitive Survey. Boston: Little, Brown and Company.

Moglia, Ronald Filiberti and Jon Knowles, eds. (1997). All About Sex: A

Family Resource on Sex and Sexuality. New York: Three Rivers Press.

Mosher, Donald L and Susan G. Vonderheide. (1985). "Contributions of sex guilt and masturbation guilt to women's contraceptive attitudes and use." The Journal of Sex Research, 21(1), 24-39.

Mecklenburger, Ralph. Our Religious Brains. Woodstock, VT: Jewish Lights Publishing, 2012

Naskar, Abhijit. "The Art of Neuroscience in Everything", 2015

Naskar, Abhijit. "Biopsy of Religions: Neuroanalysis towards Universal Tolerance", 2016

Naskar, Abhijit. "What is Mind?", 2016

Naskar, Abhijit. "Love, God & Neurons: Memoir of a scientist who found himself by getting lost", 2016

Naskar, Abhijit. "Principia Humanitas", 2017

Naskar, Abhijit. "We Are All Black: A Treatise on Racism", 2017

Naskar, Abhijit. "The Bengal Tigress: A Treatise on Gender Equality", 2017

Naskar, Abhijit. "Either Civilized or Phobic: A Treatise on Homosexuality", 2017

Ortigue S & Bianchi-Demicheli F (2007). Interactions between human sexual arousal and sexual desire: a challenge for social neuroscience. Revue Medicale Suisse 3.

Ortigue S, Bianchi-Demicheli F de C, Hamilton AF & Grafton ST (2007). The neural basis of love as a subliminal prime: An event-related functional magnetic resonance imaging study. Journal of Cognitive Neuroscience 19.

Ortigue S, Bianchi-Demicheli F, Patel N, Frum C & Lewis JW (2010). Neuroimaging of love: fMRI meta-analysis evidence toward new perspectives in sexual medicine. Journal of Sexual Medicine 7.

Ortigue S, Patel N & Bianchi-Demicheli F (2009). New electroencephalogram (EEG) neuroimaging methods of analyzing brain activity applicable to the study of human sexual response. Journal of Sexual Medicine 6.

Owuamanam, D. O. (1984). Adolescents' perception of polygamous family and its relationship to self-concept. International Journal of Psychology, 19, 593-598.

Rocca, M. A., Tortorella, P., Ceccarelli, A., Falini, A., Tango, D., Scotti, G., Comi, G. & Fillipi, M. (2008) The "mirror-neuron system" in MS: A 3 tesla fMRI study. Neurology 70(4).

Rochat, M. J., Caruana, F., Jezzini, A., Escola, L., Intskirveli, I., Grammont, F., Gallese, V., Rizzolatti, G. & Umiltà, M.

A. (2010) Responses of mirror neurons in area F5 to hand and tool grasping observation. Experimental Brain Research 204(4).

Rochat, M. J., Serra, E., Fadiga, L. & Gallese, V. (2008) The evolution of social cognition: Goal familiarity shapes monkeys' action understanding. Current Biology 18(3).

Rochat, P. (1998) Self-perception and action in infancy. Experimental Brain Research 123.

Rosenbaum, D. (1991) Human motor control. Academic Press.

Roth, T. L. (2012) Epigenetics of neurobiology and behavior during development and adulthood. Developmental Psychobiology 54(6). doi: 10.1002/ dev.20550.

Rushworth, M. F., Mars, R. B. & Sallet, J. (2013) Are there specialized circuits for social cognition and are they unique to humans? Current Opinion in Neurobiology 23(3).

Russell, J. L., Lyn, H., Schaeffer, J. A. & Hopkins, W. D. (2011) The role of socio- communicative rearing environments in the development of social and physical cognition in apes. Developmental Science 14(6).

Smith, Thomas (2011). Romantic Love. Essays in Philosophy, 12(1), 68–92.

Soble, Alan (1987). The Unity of Romantic Love. In Philosophy and Theology, 1(4), 374– 97. Reprinted in Alan Soble (Ed.), Sex, Love and Friendship: Studies of the Society for the Philosophy of Sex and Love (385– 402). Rodopi. http://dx.doi.org/10.5840/philtheol19871413

Shepard, L. D. (2013). The impact of polygamy on women's mental health: A systematic review. Epidemiology and psychiatric sciences, 22, 47- 62.

Swanson, R. B., Masssey, R. H., & Payne, I. R. (1972). Ordinal position, family size, and personal adjustment. Journal of Psychology, 81, 51–58.

Solomon, Robert (1988.) About Love: Reinventing Romance for Our Times. Simon & Schuster.

Tardiff, Suzette D. 1994 Relative Energetic Costs of Infant Care in Small Bodied Neotropical Primates and Its Relation to Infant Care Patterns. American Journal of Primatology 34:133-143.

Tattersall, Ian 1976 Group Structure and Activity Rhythm in Lemur mongoz (Primates, Lemuriformes) on Anjouan and Moheli Islands, Comoro Archipelago. Anthropological Papers of the American Museum of Natural History 53(4):369-380. 1982 The Primates of Madagascar. New York: Columbia University Press.

Tenaza, Richard R. 1989 Female Sexual Swellings in the Asian Colobine Simias concolor. American Journal of Primatology 17: 81-86.

Tenaza, R. R., and A. Fuentes 1995 Monandrous Social Organization in the Pig-Tailed Langur (Simias concolor). International Journal of Primatology 16(2): 195-210.

Tilson, Ronald L. 1980 Monogamous Mating Systems of Gibbons and Langurs in the Mentawai Islands, Indonesia. Ph.D. dissertation, University of California, Davis. 1981 Family Formation Strategies of Kloss's Gibbons. Folia Primatologica 35:259-287.

Tilson, R. L., and R. R. Tenaza 1976 Monogamy and Duetting in an Old World Monkey. Nature 263:320-321.

Valsiner, J. (1989). Organization of children's social development in polygamic families. In J. Valsiner (Ed.),

Child development in cultural context (pp. 67–86). Toronto, Canada: Hogrefe and Huber.

Valsiner, J. (2000). Culture and human development. London: Sage Publications

van Schaik, C. P., and R. I. M. Dunbar 1990 The Evolution of Monogamy in Large Primates: A New Hypothesis and Some Crucial Tests. Behaviour 115(l-2):30-62.

van Schaik, C. P., and P. P. Kappeler 1993 Life History, Activity Period and Lemur Social Systems. In Lemur Social Systems and Their Ecological Basis. P. M. Kappeler and J. U. Ganzhorn, eds. Pp. 241-260. New York: Plenum Press.

van Schaik, C.P., and J. A. R. A. M. van Hoof 1983 The Ultimate Causes of Primate Social Systems. Behaviour 85:91-117.

Vasey, Natalia 1997 Community Ecology and Behavior of Varecia variegata rubra and Lemur fulvus albifrons on the Masoala Peninsula, Madagascar. Ph.D. dissertation, Anthropology Department, Washington University, St. Louis.

Vasey, Paul L. 1995 Homosexual Behavior in Primates: A Review of Evidence and Theory. International Journal of Primatology 16(2): 173-204

Weaver, Bryan, and Fiona Woollard (2008.) Marriage and the Norm of Monogamy. The Monist, 91(3–4), 506–22.

Wahome, J. M., T. E. Rowell, and H. M. Tsingalia 1993 The Natural History of DeBrazza's in Kenya. International Journal of Primatology 14:445-466.

Watanabe, Kunio 1981 Variations in Group Composition and Population Density of the Two Symapatric Mentawaian Leaf-monkeys. Primates 22(2): 145-160.

Wickler, W., and U. Seibt 1983 Monogamy: An Ambiguous Concept. In Mate Choice. P. Bateson, ed. Pp. 33-52. Cambridge: Cambridge University Press.

Wittenberger, J. F., and R. L. Tilson 1980 The Evolution of Monogamy: Hypotheses and Evidence. Annual Review of Ecology and Systematics 11: 197-232.

Wolpoff, Milford H. 1996 Human Evolution. 1996-1997 edition. New York: McGraw Hill Companies Inc., College Custom Press.

Woolfenden, G. E., and J. W. Fitzpatrick 1978 The Inheritence of Territory in Group Breeding Birds. Bioscience 28:104-108.

Wrangham, Richard W. 1980 An Ecological Model of Female-Bonded Primate Groups. Behaviour 75:262-300.

Wright, Patricia C. 1981 The Night Monkey, Genus Aotus. In Ecology and

Behavior of Neotropical Primates, vol. 1. A. F. Coimbra-Filho and R. A. Mittermeier, eds. Pp. 211- 240. Rio de Janeiro: Academia Brasileirs de Ciencias.

1984 Biparental Care in Aotus trivirgatus and Callicebus moloch. In Female Primates: Studies by Women Primatologists. M. Small, ed. Pp. 59-75. New York: Alan R. Liss, Inc.

1986a Diet, Ranging Behavior and Activity Patterns of the Gentle Lemur (Hapalemur griseus) in Madagascar. American Journal of Physical Anthropology 69(l-4):283.

1986b Ecological Correlates of Monogamy in Aotus and Callicebus. In Primate Ecology and Conservation. J. G. Else and P. C. Lee, eds. Pp. 159-167. Cambridge: Cambridge University Press.

1994 The Behavior and Ecology of the Owl Monkey. In Aotus: The Owl

Monkey. J. Baer, R. E. Weller, and I. Kakoma, eds. Pp. 97-112. New York: Academic Press.

1996 Demography and Life-History of Free-Ranging Propithecus diadema edwardsi in Ranomafana National Park, Madagascar. International Journal of Primatology 16(5): 835-854.

Wright, P. C, and M. Randrimanantena 1989 Comparative Ecology of Three Sympatric Bamboo Lemurs in Madagascar. American Journal of Physical Anthropology 78(2):327

WISE MATING